Contents

Third Edition

Copyright © 1966, 1990, 2007 by Alfred Publishing Co., Inc.
All rights reserved. Printed in USA.

Cover guitar photo courtesy of Taylor Guitars.

Alfred Publishing Co., Inc.
16320 Roscoe Blvd., Suite 100
P.O. Box 10003
Van Nuys, CA 91410-0003
alfred.com

Book
ISBN-10: 0-7390-4793-0   ISBN-13: 978-0-7390-4793-4
Book and CD
ISBN-10: 0-7390-4794-9   ISBN-13: 978-0-7390-4794-1
Book and DVD
ISBN-10: 0-7390-4888-0   ISBN-13: 978-0-7390-4888-7
DVD
ISBN-10: 0-7390-4938-0   ISBN-13: 978-0-7390-4938-9

W9-CNN-785

The Parts of Your Guitar

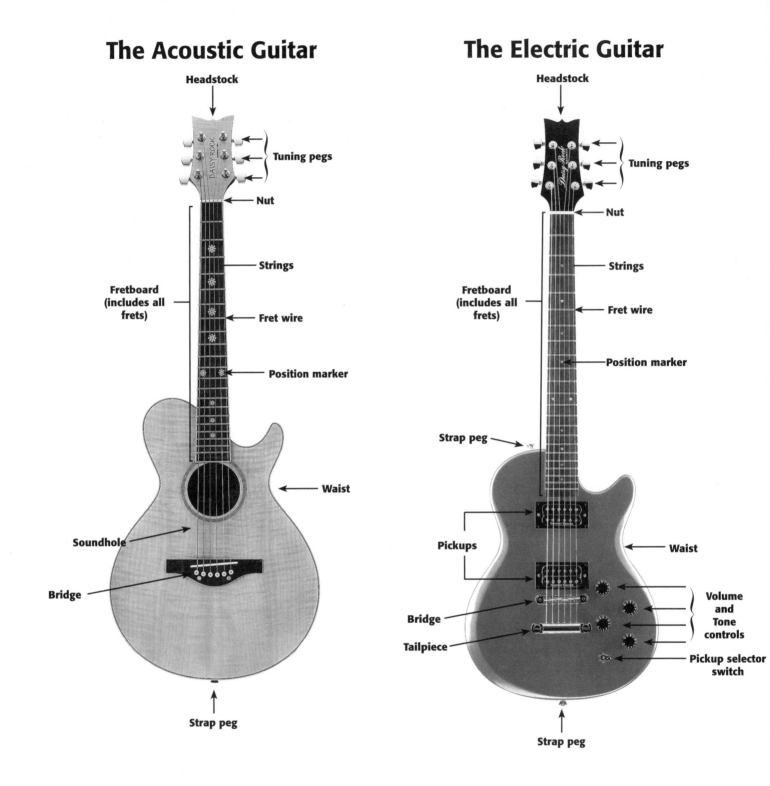

The Acoustic Guitar

- Headstock
- Tuning pegs
- Nut
- Strings
- Fretboard (includes all frets)
- Fret wire
- Position marker
- Waist
- Soundhole
- Bridge
- Strap peg

The Electric Guitar

- Headstock
- Tuning pegs
- Nut
- Strings
- Fret wire
- Position marker
- Strap peg
- Pickups
- Waist
- Bridge
- Tailpiece
- Volume and Tone controls
- Pickup selector switch
- Strap peg

Steel Strings and Nylon Strings

Steel strings are found on both acoustic and electric guitars. They have a bright and brassy sound.
Nylon strings are usually found on classical and flamenco guitars. They have a mellow, delicate sound.
Nylon strings are often easier for beginners to play because they are easier on the fingers than steel strings.

ow to Hold Your Guitar

Hold your guitar in a position that is most comfortable for you.
Some positions are shown below.

When playing, keep your left wrist away from the
fingerboard. This will allow your fingers to be in a
better position to finger the chords. Press your fingers
firmly, but make certain they do not touch the
neighboring strings.

Sitting.

Sitting with legs crossed.

The guitar is strummed with the right hand. You may
use a guitar pick or your thumb. Strum all chords in a
downward motion unless otherwise indicated.

Standing with strap.

The Right Hand

To *strum* means to play the strings with your right hand by brushing quickly across them. There are two common ways of strumming the strings. One is with a pick, and the other is with your fingers.

Strumming with a Pick

Hold the pick between your thumb and index finger. Hold it firmly, but don't squeeze it too hard.

Strum from the 6th string (the thickest, lowest-sounding string) to the 1st string (the thinnest, highest-sounding string).

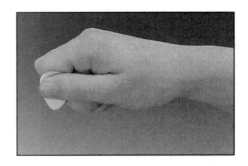

Important: Strum by mostly moving your wrist, not just your arm. Use as little motion as possible. Start as close to the top string as you can, and never let your hand move past the edge of the guitar.

Start near the top string.

Move mostly your wrist, not just your arm. Finish near the bottom string.

Strumming with Your Fingers

Decide if you feel more comfortable strumming with the side of your thumb or the nail of your index finger. The strumming motion is the same with the thumb or finger as it is when using the pick.
Strum from the 6th string (the thickest, lowest-sounding string) to the 1st string (the thinnest, highest-sounding string).

Strumming with the thumb.

Strumming with the index finger.

The Left Hand

Proper Left Hand Position

Learning to use your left hand fingers starts with a good hand position. Place your hand so your thumb rests comfortably in the middle of the back of the neck. Position your fingers on the front of the neck as if you are gently squeezing a ball between them and your thumb. Keep your elbow in and your fingers curved.

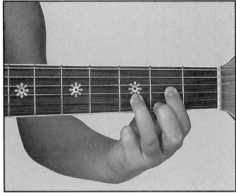

Keep elbow in and fingers curved.

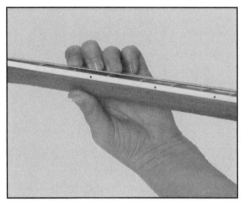

Position fingers as if you are gently squeezing a ball between your fingertips and thumb.

Placing a Finger on a String

When you press a string with a left hand finger, make sure you press firmly with the tip of your finger and as close to the fret wire as you can without actually being right on it. Short fingernails are important! This will create a clean, bright tone.

Right!
Finger presses the string down near the fret without actually being on it.

Wrong!
Finger is too far from fret wire; tone is "buzzy" and indefinite.

Wrong!
Finger is on top of fret wire; tone is muffled and unclear.

How to Tune Your Guitar

The six strings of the guitar are the same pitches as the six notes shown on the piano in the following illustration:

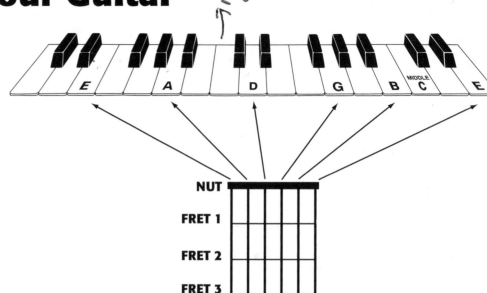

Tuning the Guitar to Itself

Tune the 6th string to E on the piano. If no piano is available, approximate E as best you can and proceed as follows:

Press 5th fret of 6th string to get pitch of 5th string (A).

Press 5th fret of 5th string to get pitch of 4th string (D).

Press 5th fret of 4th string to get pitch of 3rd string (G).

Press 4th fret of 3rd string to get pitch of 2nd string (B).

Press 5th fret of 2nd string to get pitch of 1st string (E).

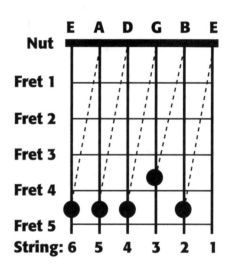

Tuning with the CD or DVD

To tune while listening to the CD or watching the DVD, listen to the directions and match each of your strings to the corresponding pitches.

How to Read Guitar Chord Diagrams

Fingering diagrams show where to place the fingers of your left hand. Strings that are not played are shown with dashed lines or "x"s above the strings. The finger that is to be pressed down is shown as a circle with a number in it. The number indicates which finger is used. This diagram shows the 1st finger on the 1st fret.

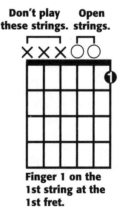

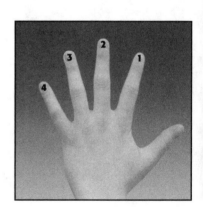

When introducing the single notes of the guitar, two diagrams are used. One diagram shows the correct finger position of the note on the guitar fingerboard along with its musical notation. The other diagram is a review of all the notes introduced on the page and also the correct fingering for each note.

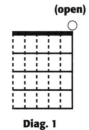

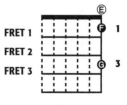

Getting Acquainted with Music

Musical sounds are indicated by symbols called *notes*. Their time value is determined by their color (white or black) and by stems or flags attached to the note.

The Staff

The notes are named after the first seven letters of the alphabet (A–G), endlessly repeated to embrace the entire range of musical sound. The name and pitch of the note is determined by its position on five horizontal lines, and the spaces between, called the *staff*.

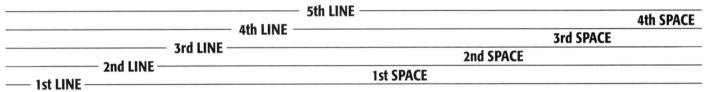

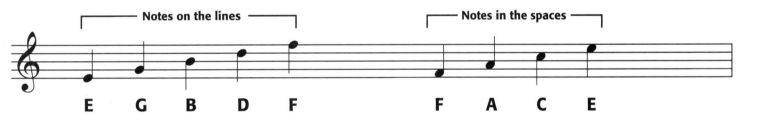

Measures

Music is divided into equal parts called *measures*. One measure is divided from another by a *bar line*.

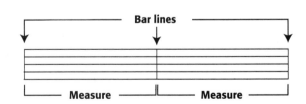

Clefs

During the evolution of musical notation, the staff had from 2 to 20 lines, and symbols were invented to locate certain lines and the pitch of the note on that line. These symbols are called *clefs*.

Music for guitar is written in the *G clef* or *treble clef*. Originally, the Gothic letter G was used on a four-line staff to establish the pitch of G.

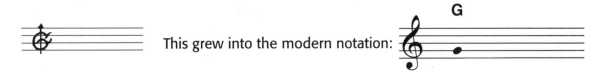

This grew into the modern notation:

8

6/08

The First String E 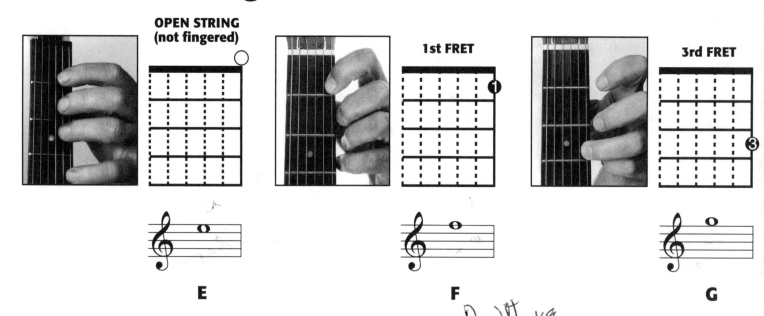 Track 2

E   **F**   **G**

Play slowly and evenly. Use only down-strokes indicated by ⊓.
The symbol ○ over a note means *open string.* Do not finger.

Dawn
Stroke

Playing with E, F, G 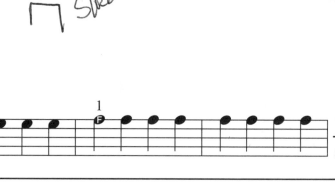 Track 3

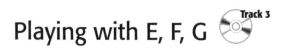

DOUBLE BAR LINE

USED TO SIGNAL THE
END OF THE PIECE

More  Track 4

9/5/08

Left hand fingers: When playing from the 1st to the 3rd fret, keep the 1st finger down.
Only the G will sound, but when you go back to F, your playing will sound smoother.

KEEP 1st FINGER DOWN   UP   DOWN

Still More Track 5

Left hand fingers: Place as close to the fret wires as possible without actually touching them.

KEEP 1st FINGER DOWN

E String

No More  Track 6

Left hand fingers: Use only the tips—keep them curved.
Left hand thumb: Place on the back of the neck opposite the 1st and 2nd fingers.

Sound-Off: How to Count Time

4 Kinds of Notes

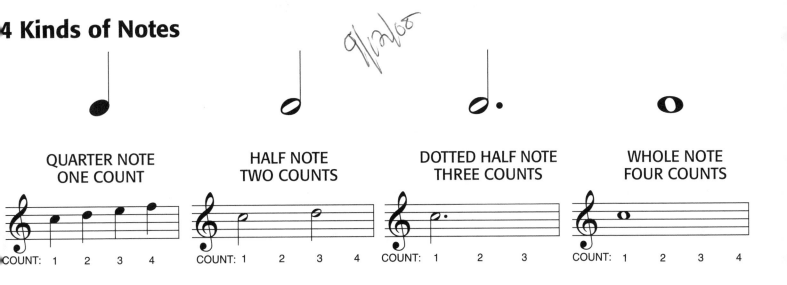

QUARTER NOTE ONE COUNT	HALF NOTE TWO COUNTS	DOTTED HALF NOTE THREE COUNTS	WHOLE NOTE FOUR COUNTS
COUNT: 1 2 3 4	COUNT: 1 2 3 4	COUNT: 1 2 3	COUNT: 1 2 3 4

Time Signatures

Each piece of music has numbers at the beginning called a *time signature*. These numbers tell us how to count time. The TOP NUMBER tells us how many counts are in each measure. The BOTTOM NUMBER tells us what kind of note gets one count.

FOUR COUNTS TO A MEASURE

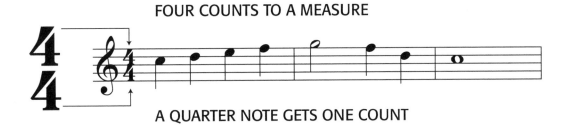

A QUARTER NOTE GETS ONE COUNT

THREE COUNTS TO A MEASURE

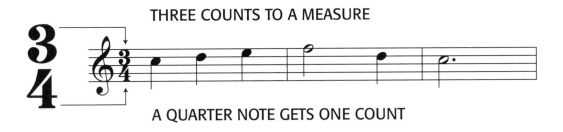

A QUARTER NOTE GETS ONE COUNT

Important: Go back and fill in the missing time signatures of the songs already learned.

The Second String B  Track 7

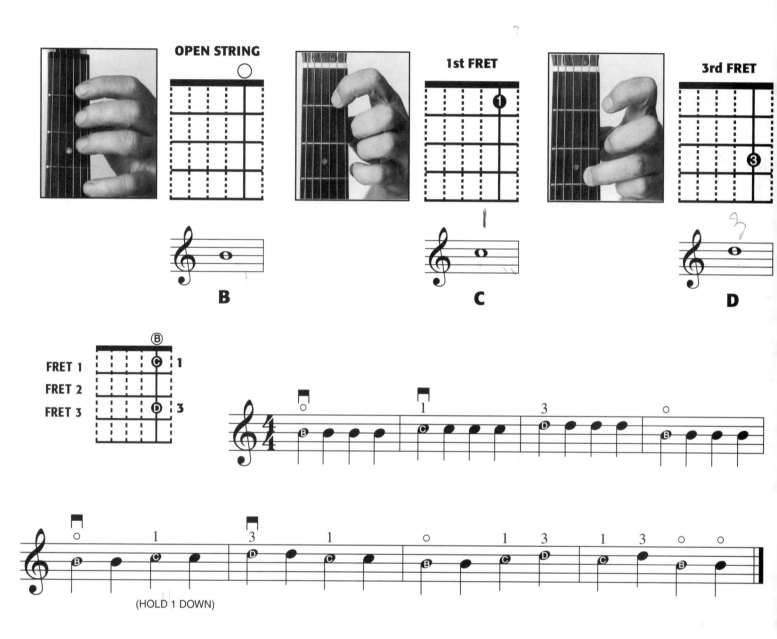

Two-String Rock  Track 8

Merry-Go-Round Track 9

9/12/08

Beautiful Brown Eyes Track 10

Beau - ti - ful, beau - ti - ful brown eyes,

smil - ing right in - to my heart. But now

where are those beau - ti - ful brown eyes? Why

must we be so far a - part?

Guitar Rock  Track 11

If the teacher wishes to play along with the student, the chord symbols above each staff may be used for a teacher-student duet. These chords are not to be played by the student.

Jingle Bells Track 12

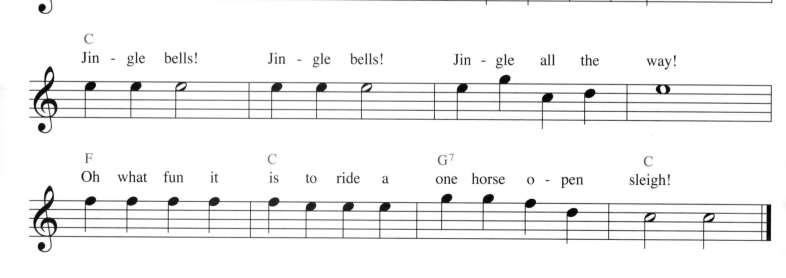

Alouette

Track 13

Traditional French-Canadian

The Third String G  Track 14

B C D E F G

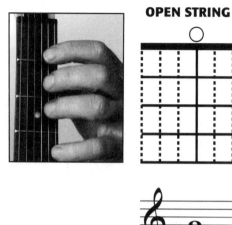

OPEN STRING

G

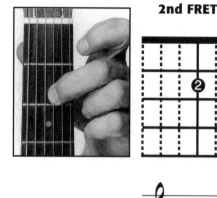

2nd FRET

A

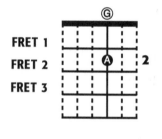

FRET 1
FRET 2
FRET 3

Au clair de la lune  Track 15

TEACHER:

Three-String Rock  Track 16

Largo
(from *The New World Symphony*) Track 17

Antonin Dvořák

18

Back to the '50s

Repeat Signs

The double dots inside the double bars indicate that everything between the double bars must be repeated.

Aura Lee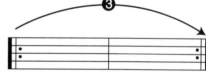

Elvis Presley recorded this folk song in a modern version called "Love Me Tender."

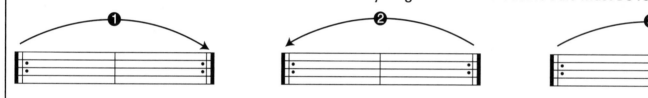

Introducing Chords

A *chord* is a combination of harmonious notes.
All notes except the whole note have a stem going up or down.
When notes are struck together as a chord, they are connected by the same stem.

(Not to be played.)

Chord Study No. 1 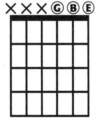 Track 20

This exercise uses two-note chords on the open B and E strings.
Play both strings together with one down-stroke.

Chord Study No. 2 Track 21

This exercise uses three-note chords on the open G, B, and E strings.

Learn the order of the strings thoroughly.
Play with the wrist free and relaxed.
Keep your eyes on the notes.

Three-String C Chord

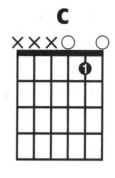  Track 22

(HOLD C DOWN TO THE END)

Ode to Joy
Track 23

(Theme from Beethoven's 9th Symphony)

Ludwig van Beethoven

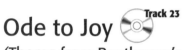

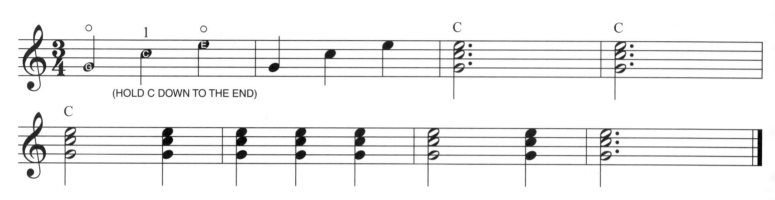

Quarter Rest

This sign indicates silence for one count. For a clearer effect, you may stop the sound of the strings by touching the strings lightly with the heel of the right hand.

Rock 'n' Rhythm
Track 24

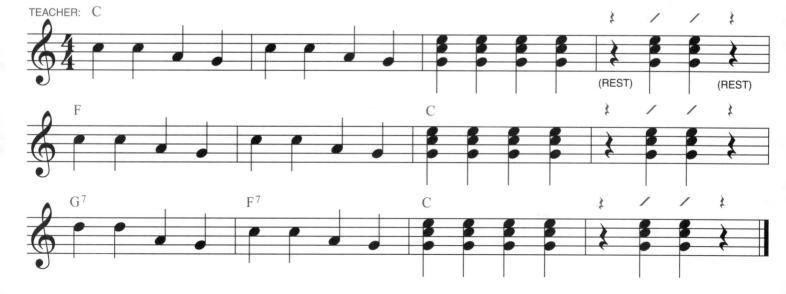

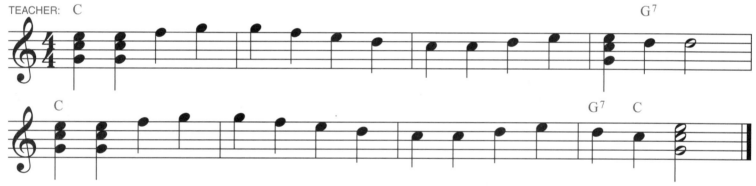

Three-String G⁷ Chord

Track 25

(HOLD F DOWN)

Two-Chord Rock

Track 26

TEACHER:

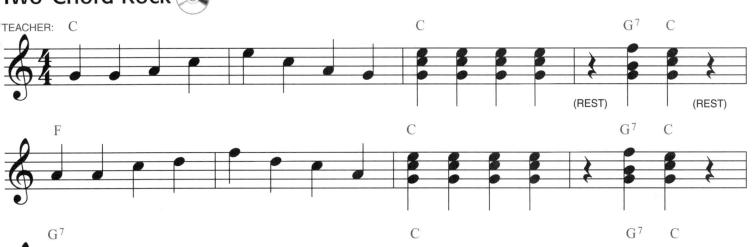

(REST)   (REST)

Love Somebody

Track 27

Here is a song for you to sing while you play the accompaniment. The slanting line below or following a chord symbol (C / / / G⁷ / / /) means to play the same chord for each line. Repeat the chord until a new chord symbol appears.

PLAY: C / / / G⁷ / / / C / / / G⁷ / / /

SING: Love some - bod - y, 'deed I do. Love some - bod - y, now guess who?

C / / / G⁷ / / / C / G⁷ / C / / /

Love some - bod - y have you guessed? You're the one that I love best.

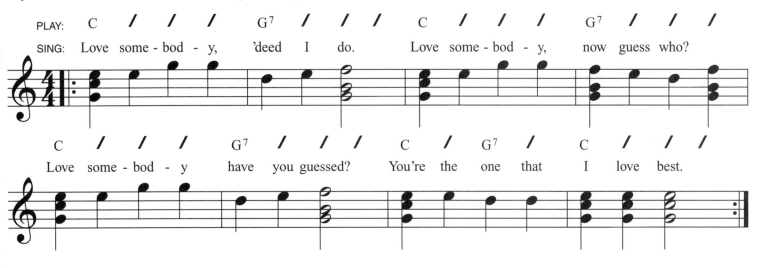

Three-String G Chord  Track 28

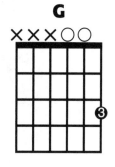

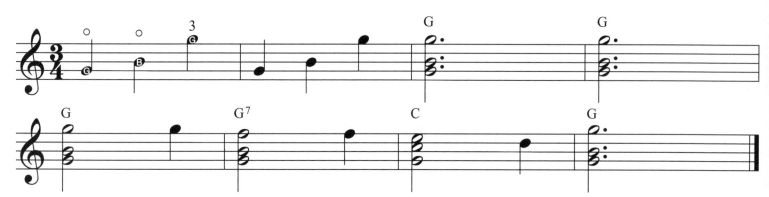

Rockin' with G & C Track 29

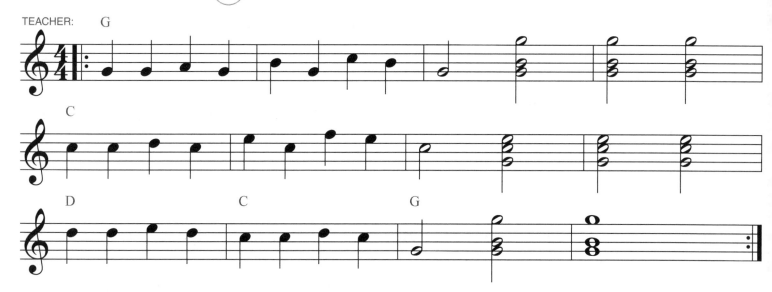

Down in the Valley Track 30

Play this song as a guitar solo by playing the music, then sing the melody
and accompany yourself by playing the chord line.

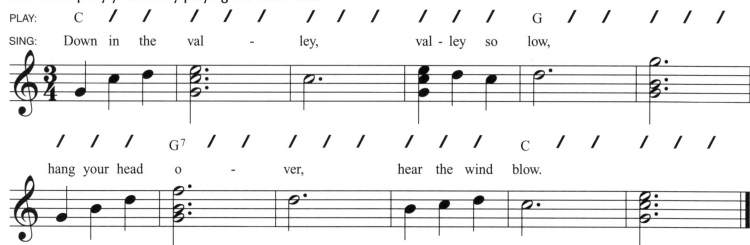

Oh, Susanna

Track 31

Stephen Foster

The Fourth String D

NOTES YOU'VE LEARNED SO FAR

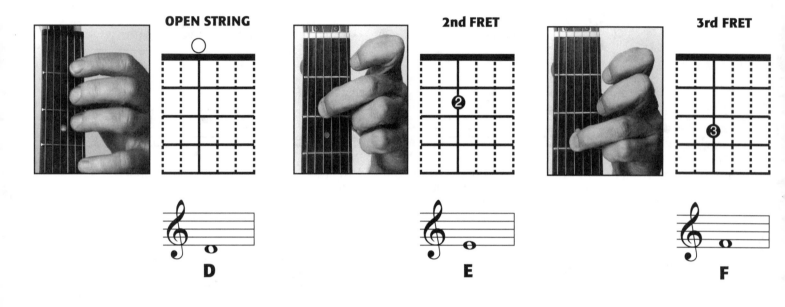

OPEN STRING   2nd FRET   3rd FRET

D   E   F

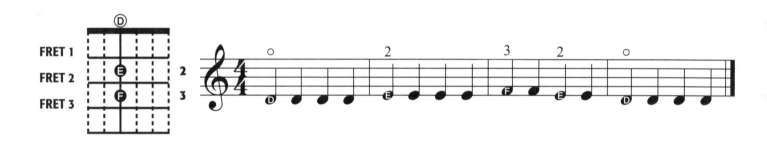

FRET 1
FRET 2
FRET 3

Old MacDonald Had a Farm   Track 33

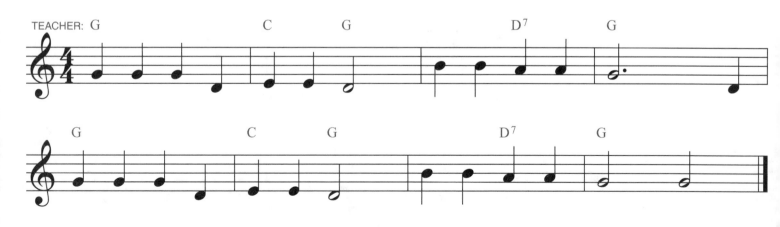

TEACHER: G   C   G   D⁷   G

Hold Sign (Fermata) 𝄐

This sign indicates that the time value of the note is lengthened to approximately twice its usual value.

Reuben, Reuben  **Track 34**

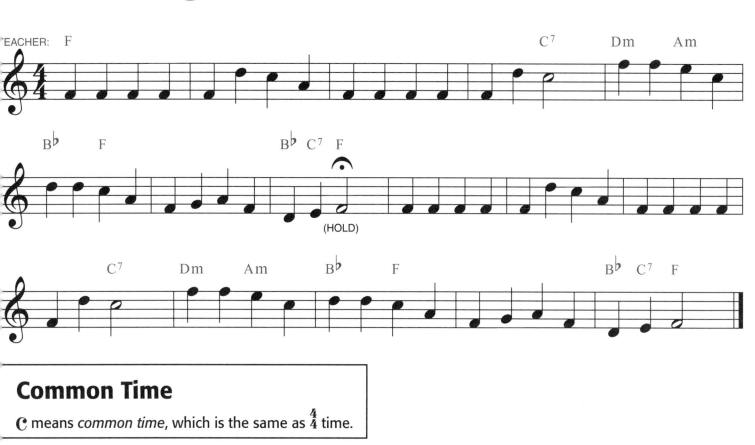

Common Time

𝄴 means *common time*, which is the same as $\frac{4}{4}$ time.

G Whiz **Track 35**

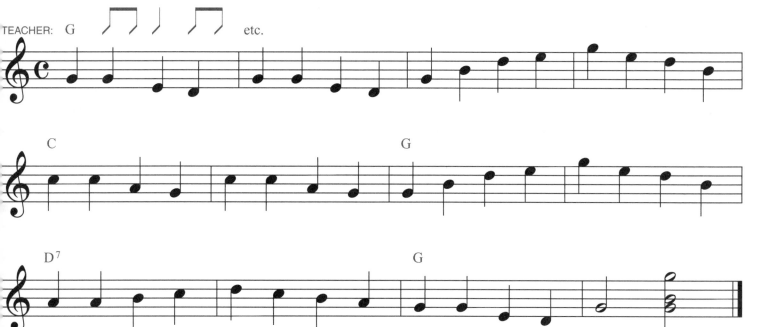

Bohemian Folk Song

Not all guitar solos are played using one form of the three-note chords already learned.
The next two songs use various combinations of two- and three-note chords.

Good Night, Ladies

Daisy Bell
(A Bicycle Built for Two)

Track 38

TEACHER:

Four-String G & G⁷ Chords

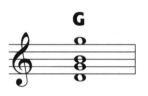
Track 39

The three-note chords you have learned so far can be expanded to four-note chords that sound fuller and richer. For the G and G⁷ chords, simply add the open 4th string.

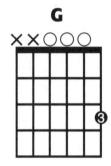

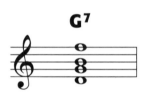

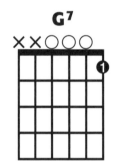

Here is an exercise using expanded four-string versions of the G and G⁷ chords.

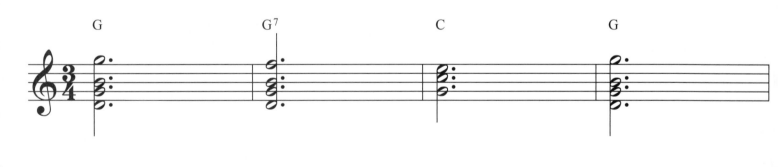

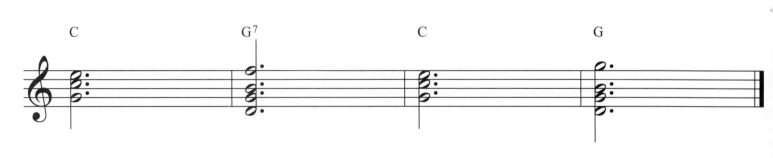

Laughing Polka

Track 40

TEACHER:

*Two thin lines mean the end of a section.

The Fifth String A

NOTES YOU'VE LEARNED SO FAR

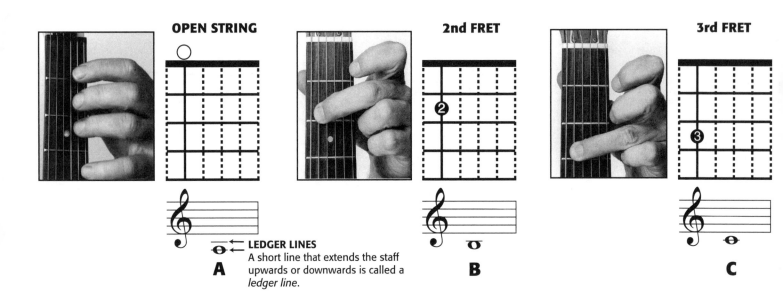

| OPEN STRING | 2nd FRET | 3rd FRET |

A

LEDGER LINES
A short line that extends the staff upwards or downwards is called a *ledger line*.

B

C

FRET 1
FRET 2
FRET 3

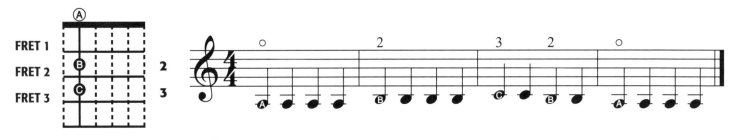

Volga Boatmen

Track 42

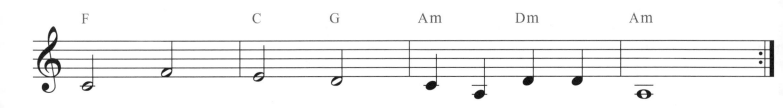

TEACHER:

Peter Gray 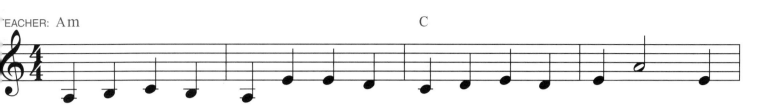 Track 43

Low-Down Rock 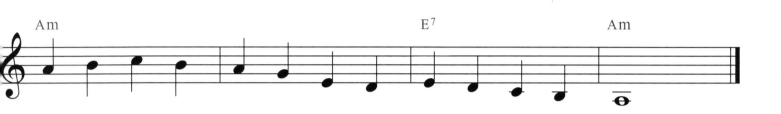 Track 44

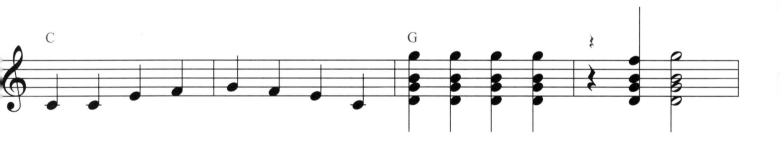

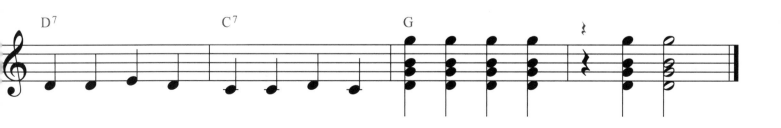

Liebesträum

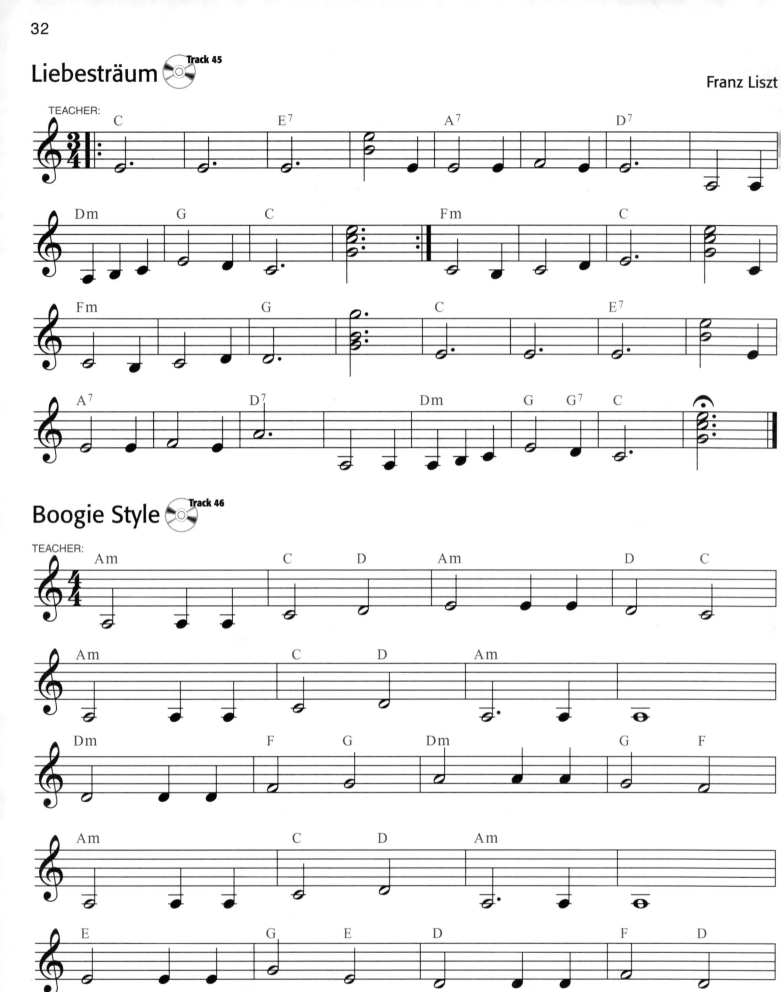

Track 45

Franz Liszt

Boogie Style

Track 46

Introducing High A

5th FRET

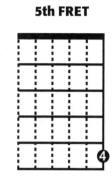

A

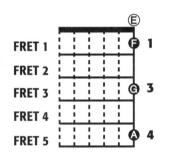

Rockin' in Dorian Mode

The Riddle Song

Play "The Riddle Song" in two ways: as a musically complete guitar solo, then as accompaniment while you sing.
Strum chords once each beat. May also be played as a duet with your teacher.

Incomplete Measures

Not every piece of music begins on beat 1. Music sometimes begins with an incomplete measure called an *upbeat* or *pickup.* If the pickup has just one beat, the last measure will have only three beats in $\frac{4}{4}$ or two beats in $\frac{3}{4}$.

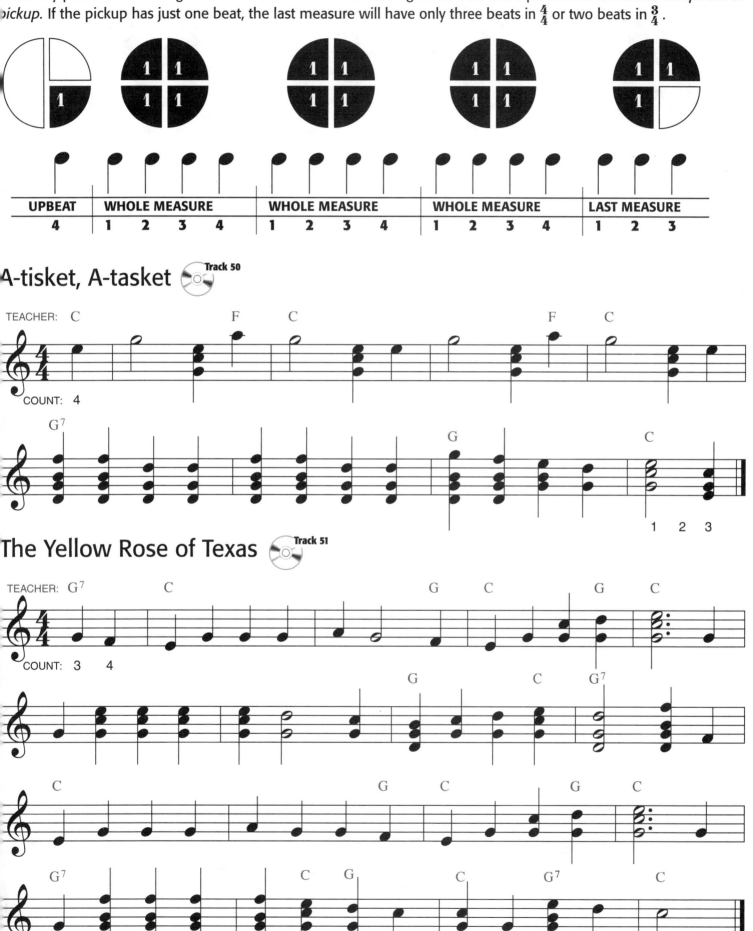

A-tisket, A-tasket   Track 50

The Yellow Rose of Texas   Track 51

The Sixth String E 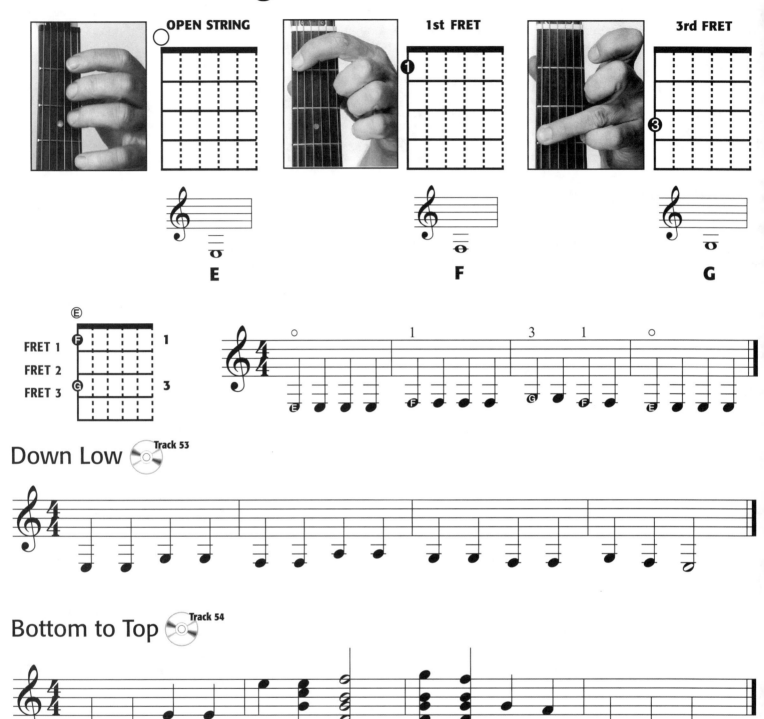 Track 52

Down Low Track 53

Bottom to Top Track 54

Review

Tempo Signs

The three principal *tempo signs* are
Andante (slow), Moderato (moderately), Allegro (fast).

Three-Tempo Rock   Track 55

Play three times: 1st time **Andante**, 2nd time **Moderato**, 3rd time **Allegro**.

The Blue Danube Waltz   Track 56

Johann Strauss

Bass-Chord Accompaniment

A popular style of playing chord accompaniments in $\frac{4}{4}$ time breaks up the chord into a
single note and a smaller chord. Play only the lowest note (called the *bass note*) on the
first beat, then play the rest of the chord on the second, third, and fourth beats.
The complete pattern is **bass-chord-chord-chord**. A variation of this repeats the
bass note on the third beat: **bass-chord-bass-chord**.

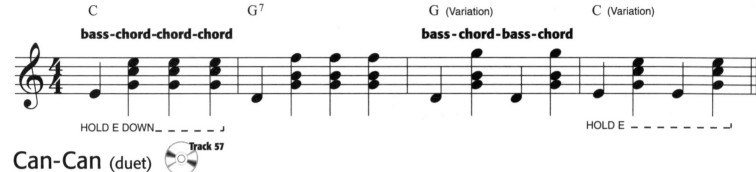

Can-Can (duet)

Track 57

This song is a duet. The 1st and 2nd parts are to be played by the student.
The teacher may accompany the student by playing the 2nd part and vice versa.
Follow this procedure on subsequent duets unless otherwise indicated.

Note: The 2nd part is written in bass-chord-chord-chord style,
but can also be played in bass-chord-bass-chord style.

Jacques Offenbach

Dynamics

Signs showing how soft or loud to play are called *dynamics*.
The principal dynamics are shown here:

p (piano) **soft**   *mf* (mezzo-forte) **moderately loud**   *f* (forte) **loud**   *ff* (fortissimo) **very loud**

Echo Waltz Track 58

Moderato

Signs of Silence

Stop the sound of the strings by touching them lightly with the heel of your hand.

𝄽	**QUARTER REST**	**= 1 COUNT**
▬	**HALF REST**	**= 2 COUNTS**
▬	**WHOLE REST**	**= 4 COUNTS IN $\frac{4}{4}$ TIME**
		3 COUNTS IN $\frac{3}{4}$ TIME

The Desert Song   Track 59
(Study in Counting)

Echo Rock

Track 60

Two tempo signs may be combined. **Allegro moderato** means "moderately fast."

She'll Be Comin' 'Round the Mountain

Track 61

Four-String C Chord

The four-string C chord requires placing the 2nd finger on the 2nd fret of the 4th string.

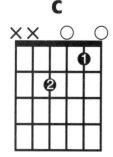

Ties

A *tie* is a curved line that connects two or more notes of the same pitch. When two notes are tied, the second one is not played; rather, the value is added to the first note.

Hold D for 5 beats.

When the Saints Go Marching In (duet or trio)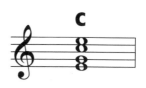

Track 62

Allegro

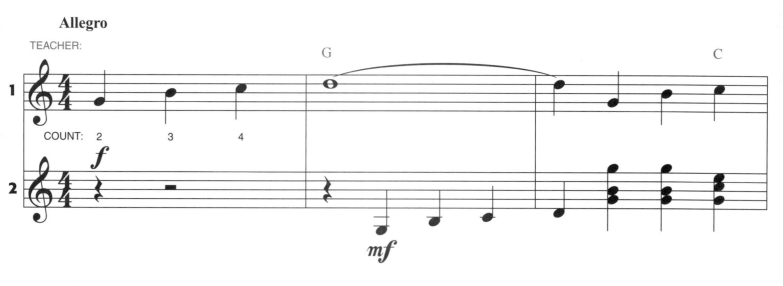

More Bass-Chord Accompaniments

When a piece is in 𝟥/𝟦 time, a popular style of chord accompaniment is **bass-chord-chord**.
The bass note is the note that names the chord (C for the C chord, G for the G and G⁷ chords, etc.).
Usually, the bass note is also the lowest note in the chord. First play the bass note alone,
then the rest of the chord on the second and third beats.

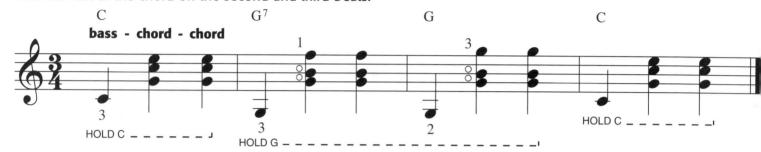

If a chord is repeated for two or more measures, an *alternate* bass note
(another note in the chord) is used to get a greater variety of sound.

Chiapanecas
Track 63

Mexican Handclapping Song

Eighth Notes

Eighth notes are black notes with a flag added to the stem: ♪ or ♩.

Two or more eighth notes are written with beams: ♫ or ♫, ♬ or ♬.
Each eighth note receives one half beat.

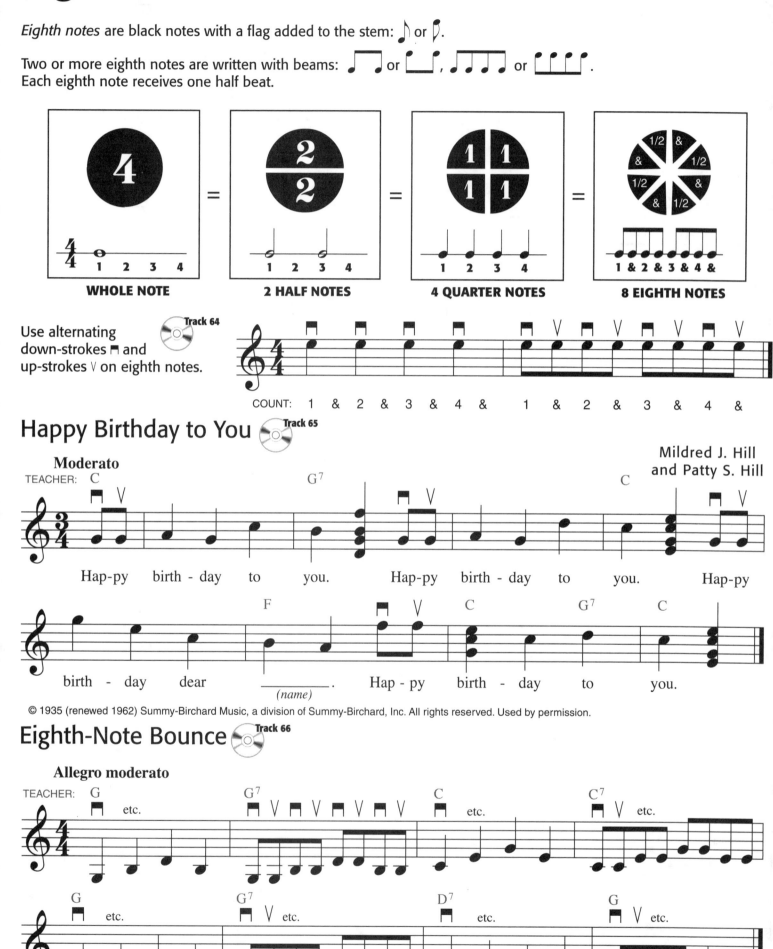

Use alternating
down-strokes ⊓ and
up-strokes ∨ on eighth notes.   Track 64

COUNT: 1 & 2 & 3 & 4 &   1 & 2 & 3 & 4 &

Happy Birthday to You   Track 65

Mildred J. Hill
and Patty S. Hill

Moderato

TEACHER: C   G⁷   C

Hap-py   birth - day   to   you.   Hap-py   birth - day   to   you.   Hap-py

F   C   G⁷   C

birth - day   dear   _____ (name).   Hap-py   birth - day   to   you.

© 1935 (renewed 1962) Summy-Birchard Music, a division of Summy-Birchard, Inc. All rights reserved. Used by permission.

Eighth-Note Bounce   Track 66

Allegro moderato

TEACHER: G   G⁷   C   C⁷

G   G⁷   D⁷   G

Walkin' Bass Rock  Track 67

Allegro moderato

More Dynamic Signs

The sign $\nearrow$ and the word *crescendo* both mean grow gradually **louder**.

The sign $\searrow$ and the word *decrescendo* both mean grow gradually **softer**.

Pachelbel's Canon Track 68

Play as a round. First player plays as usual. Second player begins when first player gets to [A].

Johann Pachelbel

Slow and stately

Annie's Song

Track 69

This arrangement can be used several different ways: the 1st part is a self-contained guitar solo;
the 2nd part can be used to accompany your singing. The student should learn both parts.

Moderato

John Denver

© 1974 Cherry Lane Music Publishing Co., Inc.
International Copyright Secured.   All Rights Reserved.   Used by Permission.

49

Sharps ♯, Flats ♭, and Naturals ♮

The distance from one fret to the next fret, up or down, is a *half step.* Two half steps make a *whole step.*

HALF STEPS • NO FRET BETWEEN

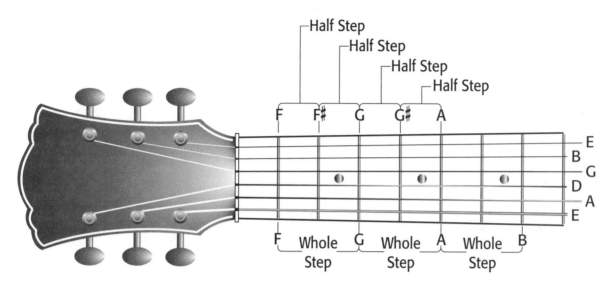

WHOLE STEPS • ONE FRET BETWEEN

♯ SHARPS **raise** the note a half step. Play the next fret higher.

♭ FLATS **lower** the note a half step. If the note is fingered, play the next fret lower. If the note is open, play the 4th fret of the next lower string—except if that string is G (3rd string), then play the 3rd fret.

♮ NATURALS **cancel** a previous sharp or flat.

The Chromatic Scale Track 70

The *chromatic scale* is formed exclusively of half steps. The ascending chromatic scale uses sharps ♯. The descending chromatic scale uses flats ♭.

Chromatic Rock

Track 71

Allegro moderato

My Melancholy Baby

Track 72

G. Norton and
E. Burnett

Slowly

* When a sharped or flatted note appears more than once in the same measure,
the repeated note is still played sharp or flat unless cancelled by a natural.

Over the Rainbow  Track 73

Words by
E.Y. Harburg

Music by
Harold Arler

Some - where o - ver the rain - bow way up high,

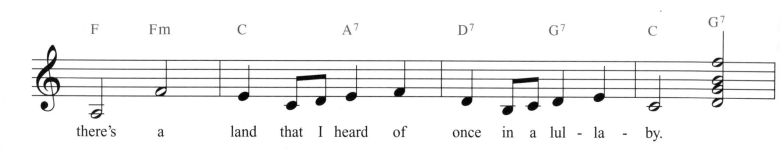

there's a land that I heard of once in a lul - la - by.

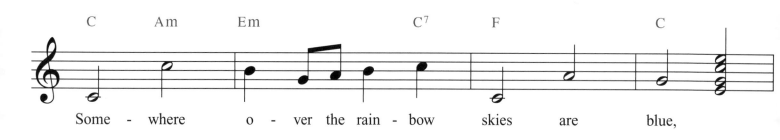

Some - where o - ver the rain - bow skies are blue,

and the dreams that you dare to dream real - ly do come true. Some -

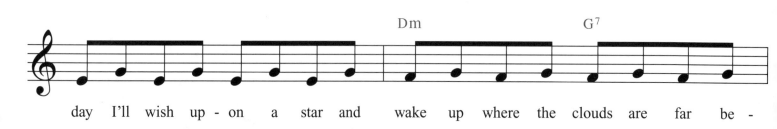

day I'll wish up - on a star and wake up where the clouds are far be -

© 1938 (Renewed) METRO-GOLDWYN-MAYER INC. © 1939 (Renewed) EMI FEIST CATALOG INC.
Rights throughout the World Controlled by EMI FEIST CATALOG INC. (Publishing) and ALFRED PUBLISHING CO., INC. (Print)
All Rights Reserved

hind me._____ Where trou - bles melt like lem - on drops, a -

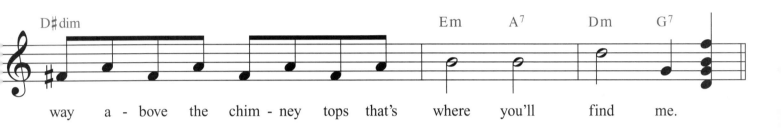

way a - bove the chim - ney tops that's where you'll find me.

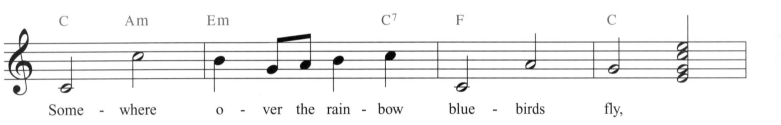

Some - where o - ver the rain - bow blue - birds fly,

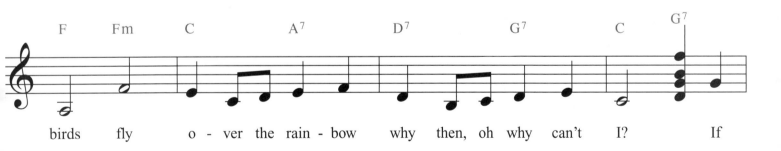

birds fly o - ver the rain - bow why then, oh why can't I? If

hap - py lit - tle blue-birds fly be - yond the rain - bow, why oh why can't I?

Four-String D7 Chord

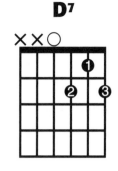

Note that the second F in measure 2 below is also sharp. Sharps and flats affect every note on the same line or space in the measure in which they appear.

Four-Beat Blues

Amazing Grace

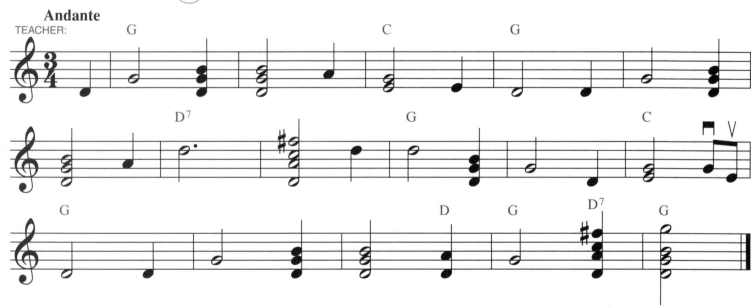

Rockin' the Bach

Track 77

Adapted from a Bach Minuet

Moderato

Buffalo Gals

Track 78

Play "Buffalo Gals" in two ways: first as a musically complete guitar solo, then as accompaniment while you sing. Strum chords once each beat.

The Major Scale

A *scale* is a succession of eight tones in alphabetical order. All *major scales* are built in the same form: **whole step, whole step, half step, whole step, whole step, whole step, half step.**

The highest note, having the same letter-name as the first note, is called the *octave* note.

C Major Scale

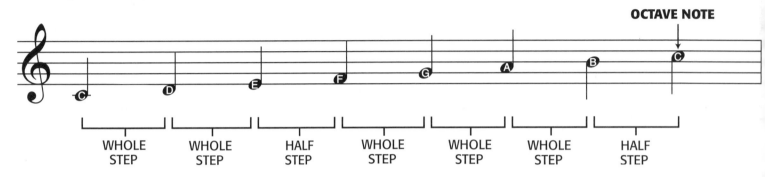

It is easier to visualize whole steps and half steps on a piano keyboard. Notice there are whole steps between every natural note except E–F and B–C.

Whole steps = One key between

Half steps = No key between

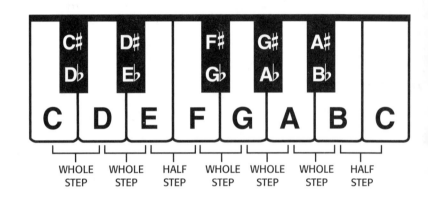

A major scale may be built starting on any note, whether natural, sharp, or flat.
Using the pattern, write a major scale starting on G.

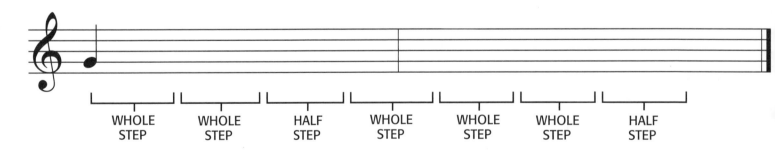

Write a major scale starting on F.

Check: Are the notes in alphabetical order?

Key Signatures

The Key of C Major

A piece based on the C major scale is in the *key of C major.*

The Key of G Major

A piece based on the G major scale is in the *key of G major.* Since F is sharp in the G scale, every F will be sharp in the key of G major. Instead of making all the F's sharp in the piece, the sharp is indicated at the beginning, in the *key signature.* Sharps or flats shown in the key signature are effective throughout the piece.

Key Signature
One Sharp (F♯)

The Key of F Major

A piece based on the F major scale is in the *key of F major.*

Key Signature
One Flat (B♭)

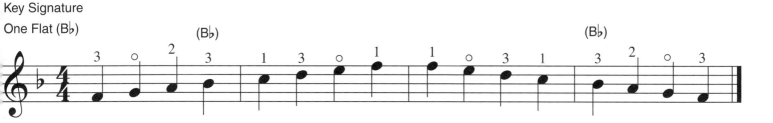

Accidentals

If sharps, flats, or naturals not shown in the key signature occur in the piece, they are called *accidentals.* Accidentals are effective only for the measures in which they appear.

The three scales shown above should be practiced every day. Students who do this will have little difficulty playing selections written in C major, G major, and F major.

Eighth Rests

This is an *eighth rest*.
It means to rest for the value of an eighth note.

Single eighth notes are often used with eighth rests:

COUNT: 1   &

Clap or tap the following rhythm:

COUNT: 1 & 2 & 3 & 4 &

Eighth Rest Exercise No. 1   Track 79

When playing a fingered note, the sound is cut off by releasing the pressure
of the finger on the string. When playing an open note, the sound is cut off
by touching the string with either a left hand finger or the heel of the right hand.

Eighth Rest Exercise No. 2   Track 80

Eighth rests may also appear on downbeats. This creates no problem
if the student marks the downbeat by tapping the foot or mentally counting.

COUNT: 1 & 2 & 3 & 4 &   etc.

Eighth Rest Exercise No. 3   Track 81

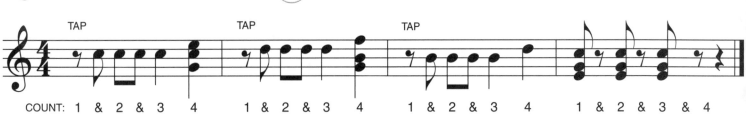

COUNT: 1 & 2 & 3   4   1 & 2 & 3   4   1 & 2 & 3   4   1 & 2 & 3 & 4

Bill Bailey  Track 82

Moderate ragtime tempo

TEACHER:

H. Cannon

COUNT: 1 & 2 & 1 & 2 & 1 & 2 & etc.

La Bamba Track 83

Allegro moderato

TEACHER:

COUNT: 1 2 & 3 4 & 1 & 2 &

1 2 & 3 & 4 & 1 &

1 & 2 & 3 & 4 &

Repeat and fade

Dotted Quarter Notes

**A DOT INCREASES
THE LENGTH OF A NOTE
BY ONE HALF**

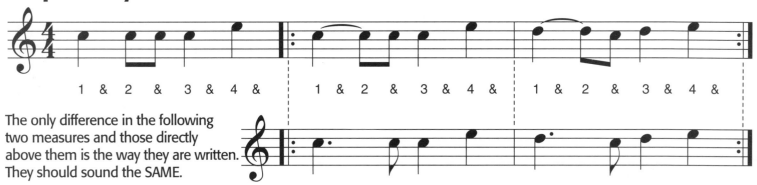

Preparatory Drill

The only difference in the following
two measures and those directly
above them is the way they are written.
They should sound the SAME.

Auld Lang Syne Track 84

ingin' in the Rain

Track 85

Lyric by
rthur Freed

Music by
Nacio Herb Brown

Moderately

I'm sing - in' in the rain, just sing - in' in the rain. What a glo - ri - ous feel - ing, I'm hap - py a - gain. I'm laugh - ing at clouds, so dark up a - bove. The sun's in my heart, and I'm read - y for love. Let the storm - y clouds chase ev - 'ry - one from the place. Come on with the rain; I've a smile on my face. I'll walk down the lane with a hap - py re - frain, and sing - in', just sing - in' in the rain.

© 1929 (Renewed) METRO-GOLDWYN-MAYER INC.
All Rights Controlled by EMI ROBBINS CATALOG INC. (Publishing) and ALFRED PUBLISHING CO., INC. (Print)
All Rights Reserved

Take Me Home, Country Roads

Track 86

This country classic is arranged as a duet. The student should learn both parts.

Words and Music by
Bill Danoff, Taffy Nivert
and John Denver

Bright country tempo

Al - most heav - en, West Vir - gin - ia,
All my mem - 'ries gath - er 'round her,

Blue Ridge Moun - tains, Shen - an - do - ah Riv - er.
min - er's la - dy, stran - ger to blue wa - ter.

Life is old there, old - er than the trees, young - er than the
Dark and dust - y, paint - ed on the sky, mist - y taste of

moun - tains, grow - in' like a breeze. } Coun - try roads, take me
moon - shine, tear - drop in my eye.

home to the place I be - long:

© 1971 CHERRY LANE MUSIC PUBLISHING CO., INC.
International Copyright Secured
All Rights Reserved   Used by Permission

D.S al Fine means repeat back to the 𝄋 (*dal segno* sign), then play until the word *Fine*, which indicates the end.

CERTIFICATE OF PROMOTION

ALFRED'S BASIC
GUITAR METHOD 1

This certifies that

_____

has mastered
Alfred's Basic Guitar Method 1
and is promoted to
Alfred's Basic Guitar Method 2.

Teacher _____

Date _____